LILL

D R

MOTHER'S

FATHER'S DAY

PROGRAM BUILDER NO.10
CREATIVE RESOURCES FOR PROGRAM DIRECTORS

COMPILED BY KIM MESSER

Lillenas *PUBLISHING COMPANY*

KANSAS CITY, MO 64141

Questions? Please write or call:
    Lillenas Publishing Company
    Drama Resources
    P. O. Box 419527
    Kansas City, MO 64141
    Phone: 816-931-1900 • Fax: 816-412-8390
    E-mail: drama@lillenas.com
    Web Site: www.lillenasdrama.com

Cover Design: J. R. Caines

CONTENTS

Recitations for Preschool   5

Recitations for Ages 5 to 7   7

Recitations for Ages 8 to 10   10

Adult Recitations   12

Plays & Monologues for All Ages   15
    A Gift for Mom   15
    Father's Most Wanted   17
    What If No One Ever Called Me Mama?   19
    A Letter to My Mother   22

RECITATIONS FOR PRESCHOOL

An Awesome Mom

God gave to me an awesome
  mom;
Her heart is filled with love.
She lets me know how much she
  cares
And tells me of God above.

Iris Gray Dowling

Happy Father's Day

I'll take a look around
To count the dads today.
Right now, we'd like to welcome
you.
Have a Happy Father's Day!

Iris Gray Dowling

Very Thankful

I thank Jesus
In heaven above
For my Mother's
And my Daddy's love.

Beverly Ann Hoffeditz

Sharing Love

CHILD 1: All the mothers
  gathered here,
  Listen to what we
  have to say;
CHILD 2: We want to share our
  love with you,
  For no one has your
  caring way.
BOTH: We love you! (*Throw a
  kiss to audience*)
  Have a Happy
  Mother's Day!

Iris Gray Dowling

Father

*(This recitation can be done by six
children, each holding up the appropri-
ate letter as they recite their verse.)*
F stands for fearless—that's my
  dad.
A stands for awesome—he's the
  best father anyone ever had.
T stands for truthful—I know I
  can count on him.
H stands for helpful—he taught
  me to swim.
E stands for energy—he needs
  lots to keep up with me.
R stands for loving—he holds
  me on his knee.

Wanda E. Brunstetter

Dad Works Hard

Dad works so hard for all of us
To make our home a happy
place.
At times, he feels all tense and
tired,
But tries to show real love and
grace.

Iris Gray Dowling

The Finest Dad

My dad is a big tall man
Just as I would like to be.
He is the finest one I know—
A man of truth that all can see.

Iris Gray Dowling

The Best Mother

CHILD 1: The best mother is
one who cares.
CHILD 2: The best mother
always shares.
CHILD 3: The best mother likes
to run and she
plays.
CHILD 4: The best mother loves
in so many ways.
CHILD 5: The best mother isn't
afraid of bugs.
CHILD 6: The best mother likes
to give lots of hugs.
CHILD 7: The best mother is
always loving and
kind.
ALL: The very best mother
of all is mine!

Wanda E. Brunstetter

Dad's Fan Club

Two, four, six, eight,
Whose day do we celebrate?
Dad's! Dad's! Dad's!
Three, five, seven, nine,
Who do we think is superfine?
Dad! Dad! Dad!

Rena Meyers

There's No Match

I've looked at every man
around,
No one can match my dad.
He works, and loves, and prays
each day,
And scolds me when I'm bad.

Iris Gray Dowling

Dad's My Example

I thank the Lord for such a dad
As the one He gave to me.
He tries to show what kind of
boy
That God wants me to be.

Iris Gray Dowling

RECITATIONS FOR AGES 5 TO 7

M-O-T-H-E-R

(Each CHILD *should hold up a letter.)*

CHILD 1: **M** is for one of a
child's best friends,
For the love of a
mother never ends.

CHILD 2: **O** is for the occasion
we celebrate,
For this is a very
special date.

CHILD 3: **T** is for teacher, for a
mother must be
One who teaches
continually.

CHILD 4: **H** is for happy, and we
want moms to be
Full of joy and
hilarity.

CHILD 5: **E** is for energy—moms
need a lot
When the job is fun
and when it is not.

CHILD 6: **R** is for racket, and it
is all right to shout
When there is
something special
to yell about.

ALL: Happy Mother's Day!

Margaret Primrose

Mom's Day

CHILD 1: Today is Mom's Day—
a day just for her.
She deserves to be
recognized—yes sir!

CHILD 2: She has lots of
patience—even
with me.
She teaches me
everything—from A
to Z.

CHILD 3: Mom has many
answers—for all my
needs.
She's a busy lady—
who does lots of
good deeds.

CHILD 4: I respect my mom—
and I'm thankful to
God.
She lets me know
what she's
thinking—with
only a nod.

CHILD 5: I'm glad it's her day—
when I can say
what's on my heart.
My love for her will
never depart!

Wanda E. Brunstetter

My Great Big Dad

My dad's a great big guy
  Who hardly ever cries.
He has a heart of gold,
  And let me tell you why.

He prays for each of us
  As he goes to work each day.
He shares God's love with
    others
  All along the way.

Iris Gray Dowling

Put God First

When Dad and I go out to hike
Or when I let him ride my bike,
  We have a lot of fun.

When Dad helps Grandma down
    the walk
And still gives me some time to
    talk,
  I'm proud to be his son.

But when Dad prays beside my
    bed
There's something he has always
    said,
  "Let God be Number One."

Margaret Primrose

A Mom with TLC

Your tender loving care
  Shows in all you do.
That's why it isn't hard to say
  Happy Mother's Day to you.

Rena Myers

The Best Father

The best father of all is our
  Father, God.
He performs miracles and
  wonders with only a nod.
His Father's love is shown to all
Who on His name will only call.
If only all earthly fathers could
  show such love,
As what the Father sends down
  from heaven above!

Wanda E. Brunstetter

To Mom From All of Us

We appreciate you, Mom,
  For your faith and tender care.
We're comforted in knowing
  When we need you, you are
  there.

Rena Myers

Mother of Teens

You calm our fears, you lead our
  cheers
You fit our plans, you hold our
  hands
You're always there, you always
  care
That's why we say, Happy
  Mother's Day!

Rena Myers

My Best Friend

CHILD 1: My best friend makes
me glad.
He's the best buddy
any kid ever had.

CHILD 2: My best friend likes to
play games with me.
He hugs me tight and
holds me on his
knee.

CHILD 3: My best friend teaches
me a whole lot.
The lessons that I
learn could never
be bought.

CHILD 4: My best friend takes
me to church.
I learn about God, and
Scriptures how to
search.

CHILD 5: My best friend loves
me even when I'm
bad.
He's always there for
me—my friend,
Dad!

Wanda E. Brunstetter

Mother Loves Me

(*Sung to the tune of
"Jesus Loves Me, This I Know"*)

Verse 1:
Mother loves me, this I know
For she often tells me so.
Fills our home with joy and
song,
Teaches me the right from
wrong.

Chorus:
Yes, Mother loves me; yes,
Mother loves me.
Yes, Mother loves me, she often
tells me so.

Verse 2:
Mother loves me this I know
Loving ways she tries to show
Now it is my turn to say
Happy, Happy Mother's Day.

Leone A. Browning

RECITATIONS FOR AGES 8 TO 10

Mother, Mother! Do You Remember?

Mother, Mother! Do you
  remember the lunch I took
  today?
I went to see Jesus and ran all
  the way.

This man they called Jesus was
  kind and true.
The one thought I had, was
  "He's just like you."

He spoke so tender and His face
  shone so bright,
Just like your smile I remember
  last night.

I heard of His need to feed
  those men,
How could I help their plight to
  win?

With thought of none other
  than you,
I told His disciple, "I know what
  to do."

I offered my lunch of five loaves
  and two fish
And said, "You may take them
  and do what you wish."

I thought of you, Mother, as I
  handed my lunch
To Jesus—who took it to feed
  that big bunch.

As I look back on my tiny, good
  deed,
I wouldn't have done it, if your
  words I did not heed.

Amy Spence

Giving Thanks for Mothers

*(Exercise for four children;
CHILD 4 carries a Bible)*
CHILD 1: No treasure on earth
  can compare
  With my mother.
CHILD 2: No one gives the
  faithful care
  Like my mother.
CHILD 3: That blessing God
  gave to me
  Is my mother.
CHILD 4 *(holding Bible, turns
  pages)*: I'm looking
  for words of thanks
  For our mothers.
(Reading from Ephesians 5:20, KJV)
"Giving thanks always for all
  things unto God and the
  Father in the name of Our
  Lord Jesus Christ."

Iris Gray Dowling

Dad's Day

Today is Dad's Day, a day that's
    just for him.
He dresses up in suit and tie and
    gives his beard a trim.
Then off to church the family
    goes,
Dad looks great from his head
    down to his toes.
We sit together on a cushioned
    pew
And listen to the preacher give
    his point of view.
He tells all of us kids how we
    should act,
Of course, he always uses much
    tact.
Then he tells the dads how
    great they can be
If they'll stay close to God,
    because that's the key.
Dad reaches over and takes hold
    of my hand.
It's his special day, we both
    understand.

Wanda E. Brunstetter

Doing Our Part

Dirty dishes, dirty socks,
Unmade beds and scattered
    blocks,
Mom's don't like them. What
    can we say?
Being a mother is not all play.

How can we help to even the
    score?
Feed the dog and sweep the floor,
Do our homework with a smile,
And tell Mom "thank you" once
    in a while.

Margaret Primrose

Jesus Had a Mother

Jesus had a mother, just like you
    and me.
I'm sure she held Him close and
    bounced Him on her knee.
Jesus had a mother who loved
    Him oh, so much.
She probably let Him know, just
    by her tender touch.
Jesus had a mother whose faith
    was very strong.
She trusted God for all her
    needs and whatever came
    along.
Jesus had a mother who loved
    Him more than life.
She stood by and watched as He
    died for sin and strife.
Jesus had a mother and He
    loved her greatly too,
Just as He expects each and
    every child to do.

Wanda E. Brunstetter

A Special Mother

Though your children could not
    be here
I'm sure that they would say
You're one of the very best
    reasons
To celebrate Mother's Day.

Rena Myers

11

ADULT RECITATIONS

Roses of Remembrance

These roses of remembrance
 I bring to say I care.
I thought of you today
 And breathed a blessing
 prayer.

May He who blesses earth
 With wondrous kinds of
 flowers,
Assure you of His tender love,
 Refreshing like spring
 showers.

Mothers have a special beauty
 And by God's grace they
 bloom,
Releasing heavenly sweetness
 In God's earthly living room.

These roses wilt, and they will
 die
 But leave us memories'
 pleasure.
God's love for us goes on and on
 As our eternal treasure.

Elaine Hardt

A Poem for Father's Day

I am glad there's a special day to
 say
We love our dads on Father's
 Day.
They play with us when we are
 small;
They take us to parks, the zoo,
 the mall.
When springtime comes and the
 wind is right
Dads help us fly our new red
 kite.
If we are sick, they care for us.
They understand when we cry or
 fuss.
They are proud of us and express
 their joy
At raising a loving girl or boy.
Yes, we are grateful and oh, so
 glad
God gave sons and daughters a
 special dad!

Jean Conder Soule

Faith of Our Mothers

(Sung to the tune of
"Faith of Our Fathers")
Faith of our mothers, living yet,
After church meetings, house-
    breaking pets,
Car-pooling, Little League,
    lessons at two,
None would get done if it
    weren't for you.
Faith of our mothers! Holy
    faith!
We will be true to you always.

Faith of our mothers, living
    still,
In spite of doct'ring others
    while ill.
Working long hours and dinner
    at five,
Only by God's grace are they
    alive!
Faith of our mothers! Holy
    faith!
We will be true to you always.

Faith of our mothers, passed on
    to each
Child and grandchild, nephew
    and niece.
Sharing their faith, their hope,
    and their love,
Grant them your strength and
    peace from above.
Faith of our mothers! Holy
    faith!
We will be true to you always.

1993 © James N. Watkins

*(Use the following three pieces together to honor mothers in your church.
You may want to consider giving a flower or small gift to each.)*

The Young Mother

Your children may be too young
    To memorize and such,
But we're sure they'd want to let
    you know
    That they love you very much.

The Older Mother

Through years of tender care
    You have raised your family.
We'd like to honor you today
    For guiding them faithfully.

The Long-Distance Mother

Though your children aren't
    here today
    I'm confident in guessing,
That having a mother as nice as
    you
    Has certainly been a blessing.

Rena Myers

A Mother's Day Poem

We gather today in love and praise
To thank our mothers in many ways
For all they do for us each year,
Whether they're near or far from here.
We remember them now in the words we say
And on this Mother's Day we will pray . . .
Yes, thank you, Lord, for a wonderful mother.
For caring and sharing there is no other
Better to care for us as we grow
In the loving embrace of a person we know
Will always be there to love us and guide us,
Ever watchful, always beside us.

Jean Conder Soule

PLAYS & MONOLOGUES FOR ALL AGES

A Gift for Mom

by Margaret Primrose

Cast:
>AMY
>GREG
>TOM
>MOTHER

GREG: Hey, Amy. Why did you print those big letters on that paper?

AMY: Shh! They're for a Mother's Day surprise, and I need your help.

TOM: What do you want us to do?

AMY: Well, I wrote some little poems for us to say while we hold these letters.

GREG: I get it. These are supposed to spell the word "Mother." You're just copying what Miss Gray's class is doing for the program this morning.

AMY: No, I'm not. "Mother" is a six-letter word, and Mom doesn't have six kids. She only has three, and I only have three letters.

GREG: So you want us to spell "Mom." But how will we learn our poems without more time?

AMY: They are only two lines apiece. You can surely remember that much.

GREG: I guess so.

AMY: OK. Here's your poem (*hands a piece of paper to* GREG) and, Tom, here's yours (*hands paper to* TOM). Want to hear mine?
>We're glad that this is Mother's Day
>And we hope you have a happy day.

GREG: That's not a poem. "Day" doesn't rhyme with "day." It's the same word.

AMY: Well, all right. How would you say it?

GREG: Oh, something like this:
>We're glad that this is Mother's Day
>And that is all I have to say.

15

But I guess that won't work because you always have something to yack about.

AMY: Stop it!

GREG: Sometimes I wish I could. How about this?
　　　Everyone thinks that I'm too yappy,
　　　But I hope your Mother's Day is happy.

AMY: Greg, you're going to spoil it all.

TOM (*reciting to himself from his paper*): Happy Mothers' Day, Mom,
　　　From Amy and Greg and Tom.
I already know my poem. I'm ahead of you two.

AMY (*looks at* GREG): We need to stop playing around. Wait! I have an idea:
　　　We're glad that you're our mother;
　　　We love you more than any other.

GREG: I suppose that will do.

MOTHER (*calling from offstage*): Greg. Tom. Amy. Are you ready for Sunday school? I'll be downstairs in a minute.

GREG (*calling back*): We're just about ready. Hurry, you guys, get in line.

(*They show letters M, M, and O in that order.*)

AMY: Let's yell "Surprise" when she gets here.

ALL (*when* MOTHER *enters*): Surprise! Happy Mother's Day! (*Etc.*)

AMY: Uh . . . we have something we want to say. I'm first.
　　　We're glad that you're our mother;
　　　We love you more than any other.

TOM: Happy Mother's Day, Mom,
　　　From Amy, Greg, and Tom.

AMY: Oops! These letters don't spell anything. Change places, Greg and Tom. Now, Greg, say your part.

GREG: Today I'll feed the dog and fishes
　　　And Amy promises to do the dishes.

AMY: I didn't say that. Mom, that's not what I wrote. And, anyway, the right word is "fish," not "fishes."

MOTHER: Greg, stop teasing your sister.

GREG: Sorry, Amy. I'm going to do the dishes for Mom. But I wouldn't mind a little help.

AMY (*in sing-song tone*): And I will give it without a yelp.

MOTHER (*claps*): I can't think of a nicer Mother's Day gift. Thanks, Amy, Greg, and Tom.

Father's Most Wanted
by Ellen Larabee

Cast:
 HOST—Male or female, age unimportant

Props:
 An easel
 Drawing matching the description in the script
 Pointer (optional)

Scene: Any place desirable

Summary:
 Done in the style of the popular make-a-citizen's arrest TV shows around today, *Fathers Most Wanted* pays tribute to fathers everywhere. While the wording is very humorous, it does point out just a few of the many things for which we have to be grateful to our fathers. It makes a nice piece for Father's Day celebrations.

HOST: Good morning and welcome to *[your city's name here] Most Wanted.* Today, we are profiling some of the most wanted men in all of America. Let's get right to it. And remember, these men may be your neighbor, coworker or someone even closer to you, so play close attention.

(HOST *uncovers a hand-drawn figure of a man both front and back views. He should match the physical description about to be given. The* HOST *may use a pointer if desired.*)

 No, we're hunting a very unique breed—Fathers.

 OK, physical descriptions: If their children are under two, look for eyes bleary from lack of sleep, a slumping of the shoulders from late night walking, and the most tell-tale signs, baby food hand prints on the back of their shirts.

 If their children are preschool age, look for eyes bleary from answering the question, "Why?" a few too many times, the word "potty" seems to crop up in conversation often, and the ever present dirty knees from playing horsey every night.

 If their children are of school age, look for eyes bleary from trying to remember algebra, let alone explain it. This one may be wearing a Little League coach's uniform under his business suit and may be ducking out of work early on school play day mumbling, "She'll be the third broccoli from the left, third broccoli from the left."

 And finally, the fathers of teenage children. These guys should be the easiest to spot. Look for eyes bleary from waiting up every weekend and from a look at the last car insurance bill. They are a jumpy lot with a noticeable lack of humor when hearing, "Hey, line 3's for you. I think it's the police." And, most noticeable of all, the lack of a wallet bulge in the pants. It's either gone all together or too thin to notice, we're not sure which. Some phrases that you may hear from these men include: "What could she possibly see in that kid?" "I swear, the box said *some* assembly required," "How much do you want this time?" "Did he look old enough to drive to you?" and most frequently, "OK, but don't tell your mother I said so."

Now, I'm certain quite a number of you out there are poised to call our toll-free 1-800-NAB-THEM number and normally we'd encourage that, *but* this time, we ask that you don't. If you recognize anyone from the above description, *do* attempt to apprehend them yourselves. I repeat, do make a citizen's arrest. Give them a big hug, a heartfelt thank you and wish them a very Happy Father's Day.

You've been watching *[your city's name] Most Wanted*. Thank you for your attention. Good day.

What If No One Ever Called Me Mama?

By Arlena Coffman

Cast:
>WOMAN—Dressed in sweatshirt and jeans, hair hidden under bandana; looks tired
>VOICES—"Mama, did you wash my pink sweater? I can't find it."; "Mama, Mama, he has my doll's shoes. Make him give them back."; "She stuck her tongue out at me, Mama."

Props:
>Laundry scattered
>Laundry basket
>Box of soap powder sitting on floor

SFX:
>Tape recording of children's voices, yelling specific things
>Dog barking
>Loud music

Setting: A cluttered laundry room

(WOMAN *enters room carrying laundry basket filled with clothes. There are clothes on floor with a box of soap. She sits on the floor cross-legged and starts to sort clothing. Children's* VOICES *can be heard offstage.*)

WOMAN (*talking to herself*): "Mama," that's all I hear all day long. I wonder how many times I've heard that word? It's just constant, day and night. I wake up hearing it. "Mama, Mama!" (*Talking to audience.*) How would you like to wake up every morning hearing that word? To open your eyes with a cat sitting on your belly, a dog that has evolved from a baby elephant kissing your throat, and a five-year-old boy shaking you, yelling, "Fix my breakfast, Mama. Is *Bozo* on yet? Turn the TV channel, Mama!"

(*Noise continues in other rooms and grows louder as they argue and yell for* "Mama.")

(*Screaming*) Knock it off in there! (*Noise subsides just a little.*) And my daughter! "Comb my hair, Mama, I'm gonna miss the bus. Have you seen my homework, Mama? Ouch, you're pulling my hair!"

And it doesn't get any better the older they get. My son in college called last week. (*Pretends to talk on phone.*) "Hello, Mama. I invited five guys from the fraternity house to come home with me for dinner tonight. We'll be there at 6:00. I knew you'd understand." No—wait, I don't have enough food on hand for six hungry boys! *(Looks into phone)* Oh, he hung up.

And my married one. Ha! She calls me three or four times a day, "Mama, how do you make chicken cacciatore? Mama, would you mind watching the kids tonight so Jim and I can go out?"

It never lets up. I swear, even the dog is against me. I'm convinced when he barks he goes *(changes voice to dog sound)* Maaa-Maaa!

My husband? My husband, you ask? Some help he is. What does he say to the kids? "Go ask Mama. She knows all about that stuff."

(Noise gets louder as children continue to argue and scream, "Mama.")

It's getting to me, the noise, the confusion. *(Lifts her head and hands to heaven.)* Lord, Lord, I'd like to get through just one day without someone calling me Mama!

(Instant silence. VOICES stop immediately. WOMAN seems startled, turns toward room where noise was coming from. Then realizing what has happened starts talking to the Lord, pleading!)

Oh no, Lord! I didn't really mean it. I couldn't live without them. How could I? What if no one ever called me Mama? What good would I be? I know it's hard at times, but it isn't their fault. I didn't really mean to complain. I don't mind being woke up so early and the dog doesn't really kiss all that bad. And besides, they only want to be near me. My little boy always wants to lie beside me for a moment, "snuggle with me, Mama, because you're so warm." It is such a nice feeling, Lord.

And my daughter isn't really complaining. She's just being a little girl, fidgety and sassy. It's a few moments we get to share together in the mornings, a time when I can touch and be near her. She's so special to me.

My son didn't mean to upset me by bringing all those hungry boys home. He only did it because he likes his Mama's cooking. At least he isn't ashamed of his parents. What if he never brought them home?

My married daughter, she only calls me to babysit because she trusts me. I never realized it before, Lord, but she must think I'm a good mother to trust her most valued possessions into my care. She doesn't want anyone else watching them.

My husband? Well, what else can he do? Of course he has to tell the kids to go ask Mama. He has given that honor to me, this is my territory and he is telling them so. Go ask Mama, she's the one who knows where the hair ribbons are and the misplaced socks. He's really giving me a compliment, only I never looked at it that way before.

It is an honor to be called "Mama," Lord! A special honor. A precious gift and I thank you for letting me be one to receive it. Not just anyone can handle it. (*Panicky*) Oh please, Lord. I didn't mean it. I'm sorry. I do love that word. Please Lord, don't take it from me. (*Crying*) I want to hear it again and again. I want it to be the last word I hear as I lay on my deathbed. "Oh Mama!" Please Lord, just once more, I really didn't mean it! How empty my days would be. I'd have no reason to even get out of bed. What good would it do? I'd have no one to be proud of my accomplishments. Please, Lord, just let me hear it one more time.

(*Noise starts up again, arguing children, very loud. She sighs.*)

VOICES: Mama, he's spitting on me! Can I go down to Cheryl's? Can I go too, Mama? Please, please? No, he went last time, make him stay home, Mama.

WOMAN (*making shooing motions, turns toward audience and smiles*): You may both go, dear!

(*Looks upward, makes "OK" sign, and winks at the Lord.*)

A Letter to My Mother
by Donna H. Turner

Dear Mom,

I'm sorry I was so gruff on the phone, but right before we talked, Jeff and I were having a go-around about the furniture; to make matters worse, my new job has my head spinning. What I really wanted was the comfort I felt when I was ten, all wrapped up in my afghan, drinking a cup of hot chocolate, and getting advice on how to handle my problems. Since I'm too far away to do that, I decided to talk with you through this letter. I'm hoping it will help me focus on some of the hard questions I don't want to look at, and thinking of your love and caring, come up with some answers.

As a kid, I wondered how you could be so sure of your belief in God. When life became rough, you always believed that things would work out. God would not put more pressure on you then you could handle. The tough times seemed to stretch you to a deeper faith.

I also wondered why I didn't feel the same way. I tried, that's for sure. I learned the prayers, I learned the Scriptures, I learned the right words to say; but it didn't feel real to me. As I say the words, "All powerful, all loving, all knowing," I gotta tell you, Mother, the words scared me. I somehow believed that I had to be this perfect Christian to deserve God's love. Then I thought about Julie Jones. Remember her? She's the girl Mrs. Tandy picked for the princess part in the third grade play. I prayed every day that she would fall and break a tooth—so she wouldn't look so much like a real princess—or get the chicken pox or have to move away. All those prayers just so I could be the princess.

Those prayers were bad enough. Things got worse. I thought I was terrible when I took money from your purse to pay off Doris Emmett. Doris was twice my size and when she said to bring a quarter or get beat up, she meant it. My eight-year old mind figured I had two choices; one to pay her money, or transfer to another school. I reasoned that God didn't want me to get beat up everyday, and there wasn't another school in our area. So it was all right to take the money. My prayers to get rid of her were none too Christian either. I hoped she would fall off a mountain, or sink in the middle of an ocean, but she never did. Vengeance is sweet though, because she was eventually caught. Her locker had become a fast food restaurant for the school roach population.

I thought of God as a Guardian Angel. My own Personal Savior; ready to come to my aid at any moment. At some point, and I don't remember exactly when, I began to wonder why God had chosen to protect me. Why was I so special? Weren't all of us made in God's image? What about the homeless, sleeping on park benches? Was God protecting them? It occurred to me that there was more to my hip-guardian avenger than I thought.

Mother, I can't tell you how many times I've wanted to believe that we can get through anything with God's help. When Jeff said he wanted out of the marriage, I couldn't believe it. I was doing all that a wife should do; I was faithful, enthusiastic, and a hard worker. What more could he ask? I had to blame somebody for the mess I was in; and God became the target. Where was God when I really needed help?

You keep saying that God wasn't to blame, and the hurt would heal; but I didn't believe you. Frankly, I wanted to scream, "No, it won't. You don't know what you're talking about. I'll never be happy again." But you were right. As I struggle with the loneliness and pain of rejection, there are times when I know that God is beside me. I still feel the pain, but with it comes small seconds of comforting thoughts.

Life is growth. Growth is life. It is sometimes painful and hard. I find myself kicking and screaming at what I know I need to do. But, for all of that, when my energy is gone and I forget that I am loved, I can feel God's presence, warmth, and love. Mother, I finally know what you have been patiently showing me for many years; that God is here, with a love that is ours just for the asking.